SPRINGTIME SURPRISES!
THINGS TO MAKE AND DO

Written by Judith Conaway
Illustrated by Renzo Barto

Troll Associates

Library of Congress Cataloging in Publication Data

Conaway, Judith, (date)
    Springtime surprises!

    Summary: Instructions for things to make to
celebrate spring, such as a butterfly mobile or a milk
carton birdhouse.
    1. Handicraft—Juvenile literature.   2. Spring—
Juvenile literature.   [1. Handicraft.   2. Spring]
I. Barto, Renzo, ill.   II. Title.
TT157.C594   1986   745.5   85-16497
ISBN 0-8167-0670-0 (lib. bdg.)
ISBN 0-8167-0671-9 (pbk.)

CONTENTS

A BLUEBIRD FOR HAPPINESS

Spring is here—and the bluebird is one of the first to tell you about it! Hang this cheerful friend in your window.

Here's what you need:

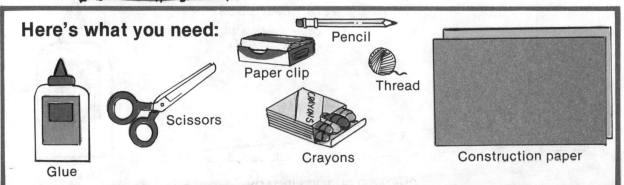

Pencil

Paper clip

Thread

Scissors

Glue

Crayons

Construction paper

Here is the pattern for the bluebird. It also shows where to place the paper clip. Now turn the page to find out how to make your bluebird.

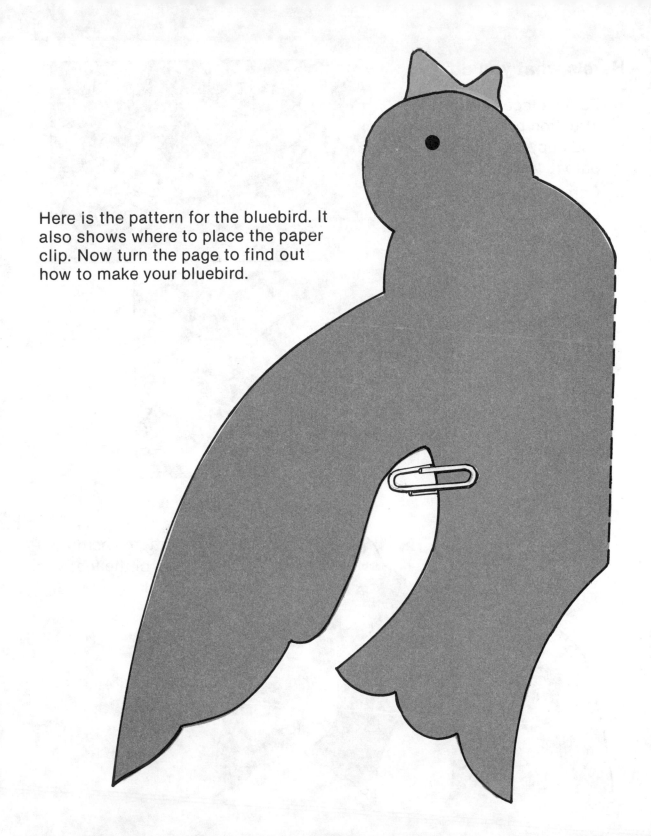

Here's what you do:

1   Fold a piece of con-
    struction paper in half
    and copy the bird pattern
    onto it.

2   Carefully cut out the bird
    shape.

3   Open the pattern and draw
    in the details of the feathers,
    eyes, and beak.

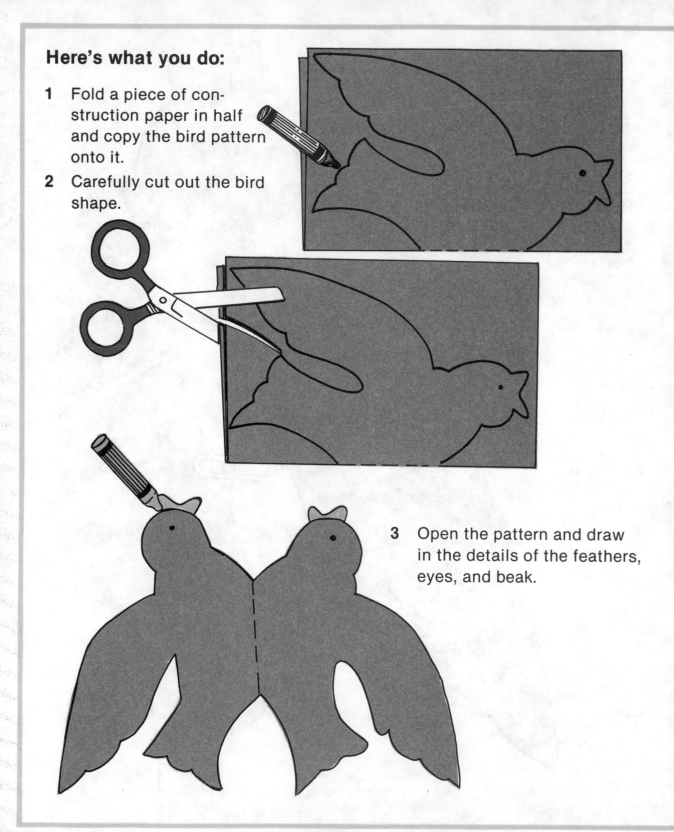

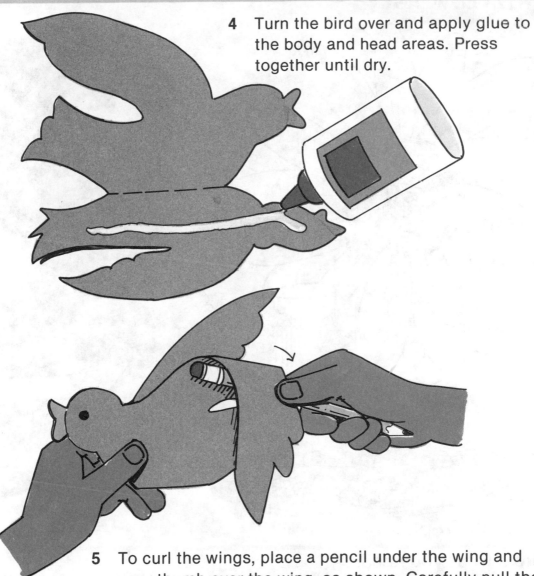

4 Turn the bird over and apply glue to the body and head areas. Press together until dry.

5 To curl the wings, place a pencil under the wing and your thumb over the wing, as shown. Carefully pull the pencil along the wing. Repeat for the other wing.

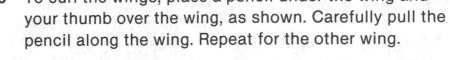

6 Tie a paper clip to a piece of string. Then clip the paper clip to the back of the bird, as shown on page 5. Move the clip as needed until the bird is balanced.

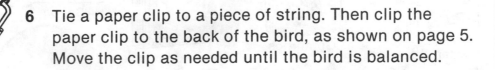

7 You're ready to hang up your bluebird. The wings will float up and down in the breeze.

CANDY FLOWERS

Here's what you need:

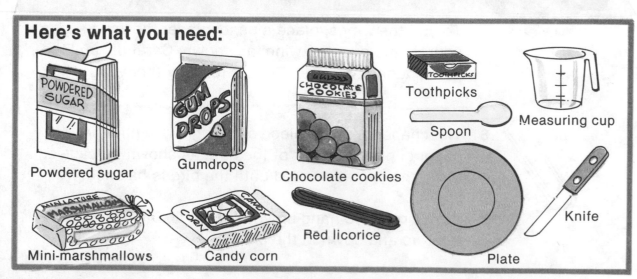

Powdered sugar

Gumdrops

Chocolate cookies

Toothpicks

Spoon

Measuring cup

Mini-marshmallows

Candy corn

Red licorice

Plate

Knife

Here's what you do:

First, make some sugar glue by putting ½ cup of powdered sugar into a cup. Stir in some water, a little at a time, until the mixture is thick and creamy.

CANDY CORNFLOWERS

Put some sugar glue on a cookie. Then arrange eight candy corns around the cookie. Place another cookie on top, like a sandwich. Slice off the top of a gumdrop and "glue" it to the center of the top cookie.

SPRING SNOWDROPS

Carefully stick three mini-marshmallows on a toothpick. Do the same for seven more toothpicks. Then push each toothpick into a gumdrop, as shown.

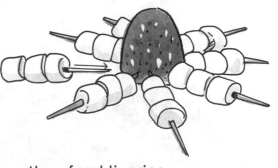

LICORICE ASTERS

For each aster you will need sixteen two-inch lengths of red licorice. Spread some sugar glue on a cookie and arrange the licorice around the cookie, as shown. Then place another cookie on top.

Keep your flowers in the refrigerator until you're ready to eat them.

LITTLE LAMB

Here's what you need:

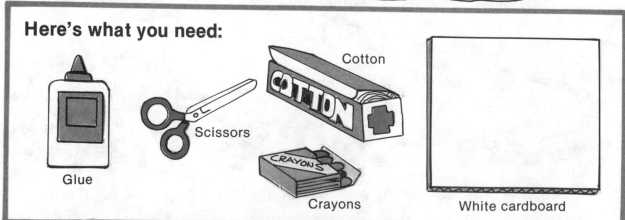

Glue

Scissors

Cotton

COTTON

Crayons

White cardboard

Here's what you do:

1 Fold a piece of cardboard in half and copy the lamb pattern onto it.

2 Cut out the lamb.

3 Draw in the legs, eyes, ears, nose, and mouth.

4 Open the lamb and glue a bit of cotton along the fold. Then glue both sides of the lamb to the cotton. This will hold the legs apart, so the lamb can stand up.

5 Put glue inside the lamb's head and press closed. Cover the outside of the lamb with glue and place cotton over the glue.

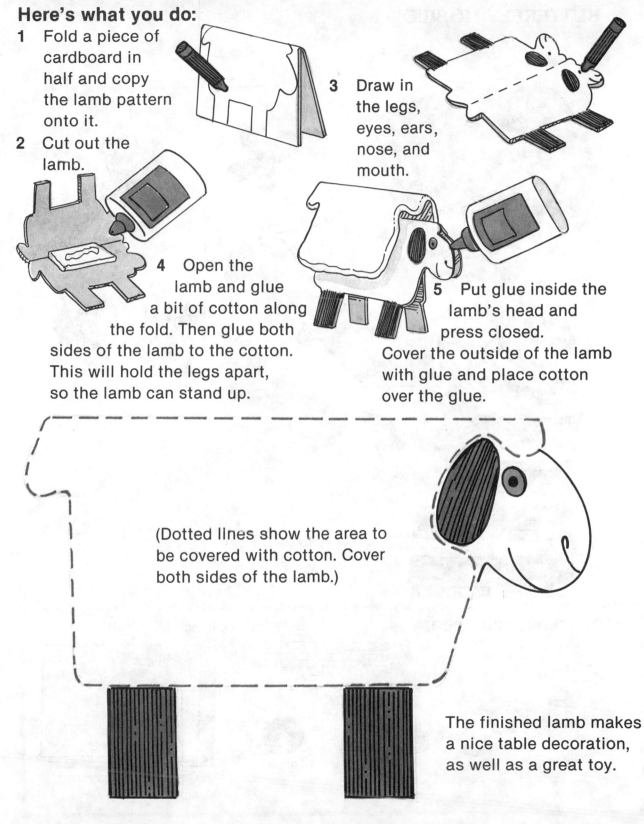

(Dotted lines show the area to be covered with cotton. Cover both sides of the lamb.)

The finished lamb makes a nice table decoration, as well as a great toy.

BUTTERFLY MOBILE

Here's what you need:

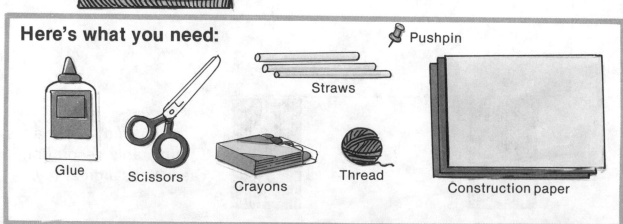

Pushpin

Straws

Glue

Scissors

Crayons

Thread

Construction paper

Here's what you do:

1   Fold a piece of construction paper in half and copy the butterfly wing pattern onto it. (You can choose one of the patterns shown on the next two pages.)

2   Cut out the butterfly.

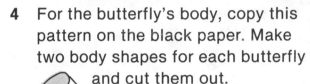

3   Use crayons to draw pretty designs on the wings. Color both sides completely. See the patterns shown on the next few pages—or make up some of your own!

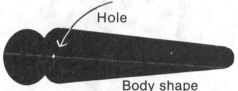

Hole

Body shape

4   For the butterfly's body, copy this pattern on the black paper. Make two body shapes for each butterfly and cut them out.

5   To put the butterfly together, glue the body shapes to the wings—one shape on top and one on the bottom.

6   After glue dries, use a pushpin to make a hole through the butterfly. (The body pattern above shows where to make the hole.)

7   Make as many butterflies as you need for your mobile.

8   To assemble the mobile, tie a piece of string to the middle of a straw. Tie another string to each end of the straw and thread it through the butterfly's hole. Knot the string to hold the butterfly in place. Now tie the string around another straw and continue to attach butterflies as you did the first one. You can use the arrangement shown on page 12.

Butterfly wing patterns

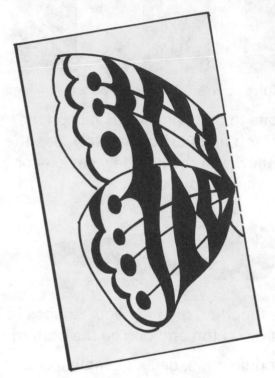

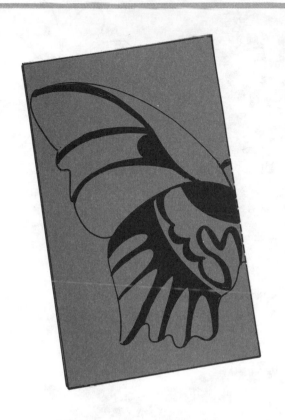

CHAIN OF SPRING POSIES

Here's what you need:

Glue

Scissors

Pencil

Construction paper

Here's what you do:

1   Fold a sheet of green construction paper in half lengthwise. Cut the paper along the fold. Then fold one of the strips lengthwise again. Copy the pattern for the loop, stem, and leaves onto the folded strip. Then carefully cut out the shape.

2   Repeat to make at least sixteen such shapes.

3   Draw some flower shapes from brightly colored construction paper and cut them out. Next, cut out the flower centers and glue them in place.

4   To make the chain, fold the stem in half as shown, and put it through the ring of the next stem. Unfold the leaf.

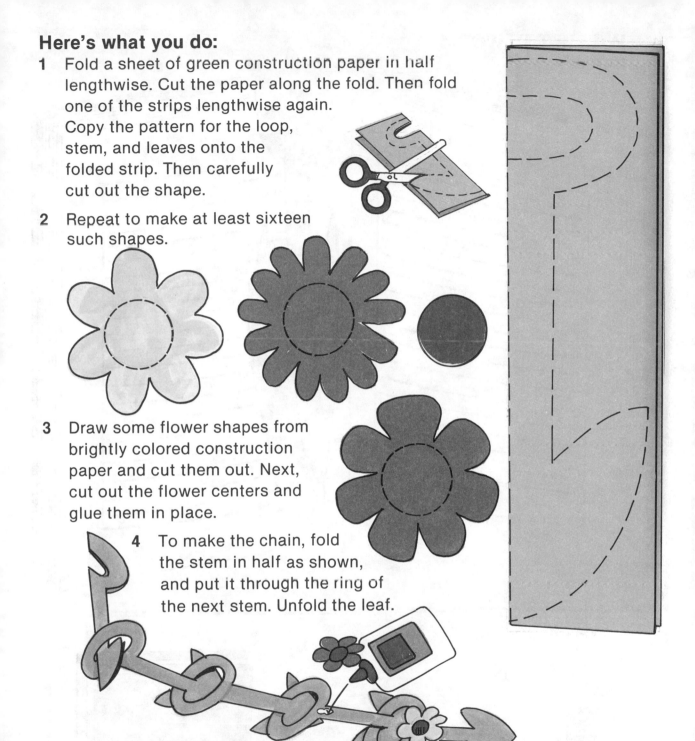

5   When all stems are hooked together, glue a flower to each stem. Let the glue dry—then hang up your colorful chain of flowers.

WILLIE-THE-WORM BOOKMARK

Here's what you need:

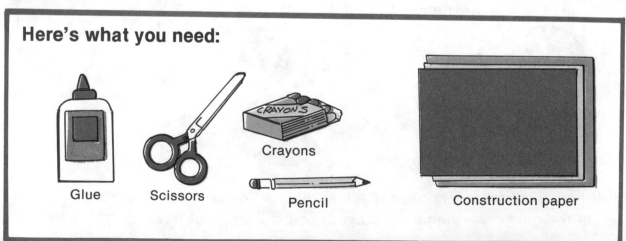

Glue Scissors Crayons Pencil Construction paper

Here's what you do:

1 Copy the leaves and stem pattern onto green paper.

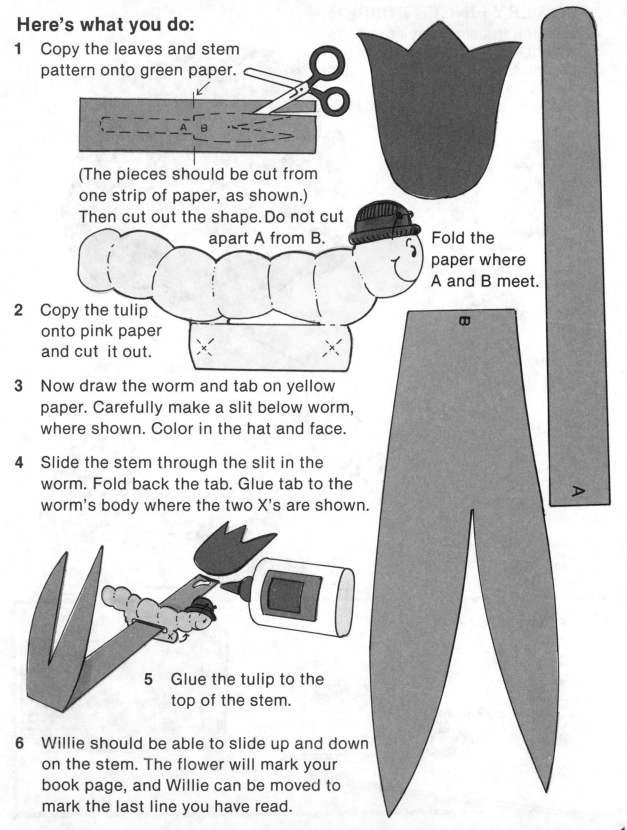

(The pieces should be cut from one strip of paper, as shown.) Then cut out the shape. Do not cut apart A from B.

Fold the paper where A and B meet.

2 Copy the tulip onto pink paper and cut it out.

3 Now draw the worm and tab on yellow paper. Carefully make a slit below worm, where shown. Color in the hat and face.

4 Slide the stem through the slit in the worm. Fold back the tab. Glue tab to the worm's body where the two X's are shown.

5 Glue the tulip to the top of the stem.

6 Willie should be able to slide up and down on the stem. The flower will mark your book page, and Willie can be moved to mark the last line you have read.

FLOWERY FINGER PUPPETS

Eileen the Iris and Tanya the Tulip are finger puppets. With these two as your stars, you can have fun making up a play all about spring!

Here's what you need:

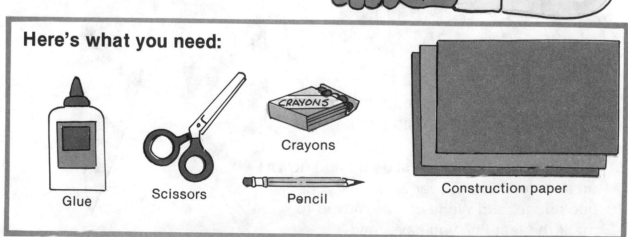

Glue

Scissors

Crayons

Pencil

Construction paper

Here's what you do:

1   Copy the pattern for the stem and leaves onto green paper. Carefully cut the piece out.

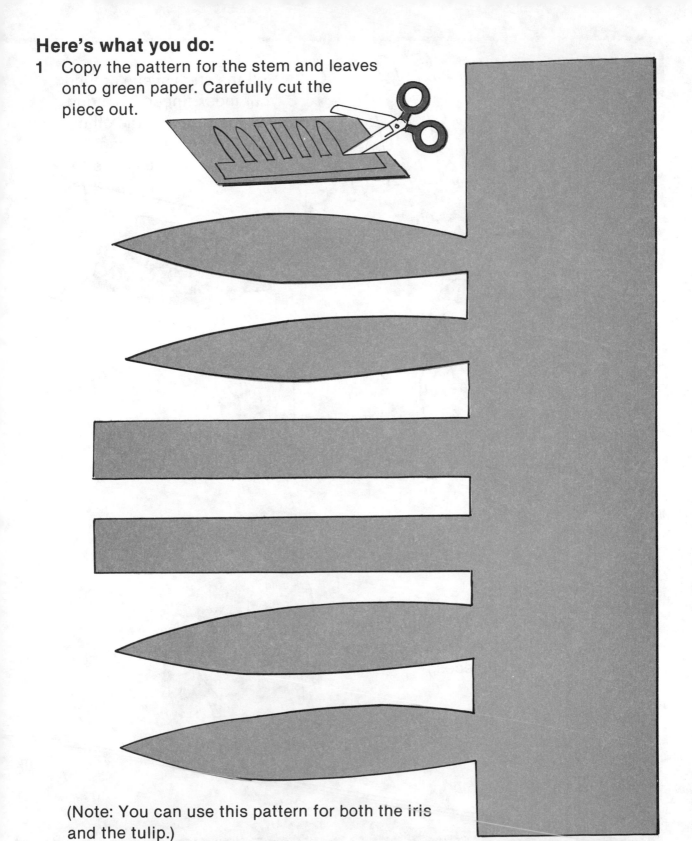

(Note: You can use this pattern for both the iris and the tulip.)

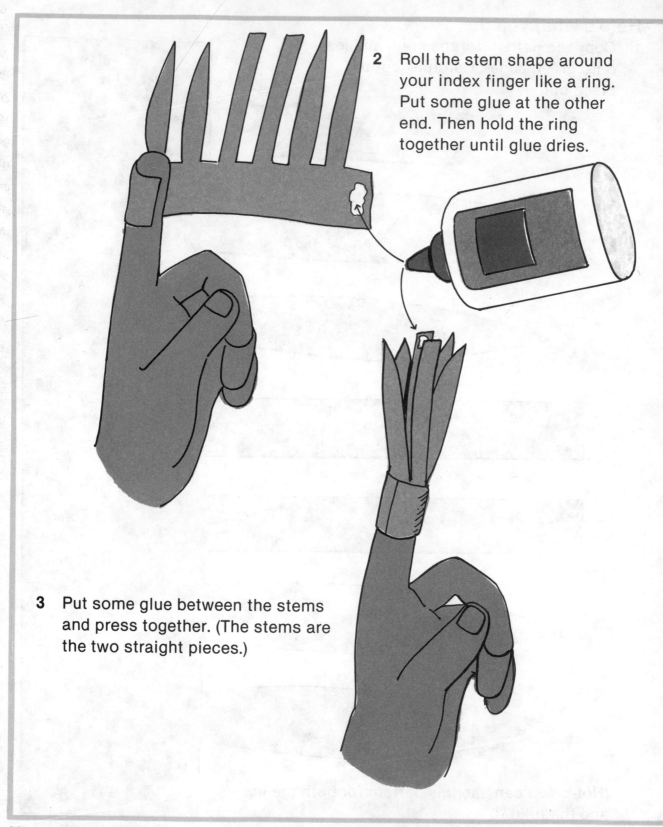

2 Roll the stem shape around your index finger like a ring. Put some glue at the other end. Then hold the ring together until glue dries.

3 Put some glue between the stems and press together. (The stems are the two straight pieces.)

4 To make Tanya the Tulip, draw this pattern on pink paper. Carefully cut it out. Draw the face with crayons. Fold the tulip at points A and B, and glue together. Then glue the tulip to the stem.

Glue

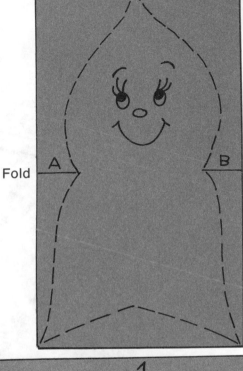

5 To make Eileen the Iris, copy this pattern onto purple construction paper. Cut it out and draw her face. Now glue the flower to the stem.

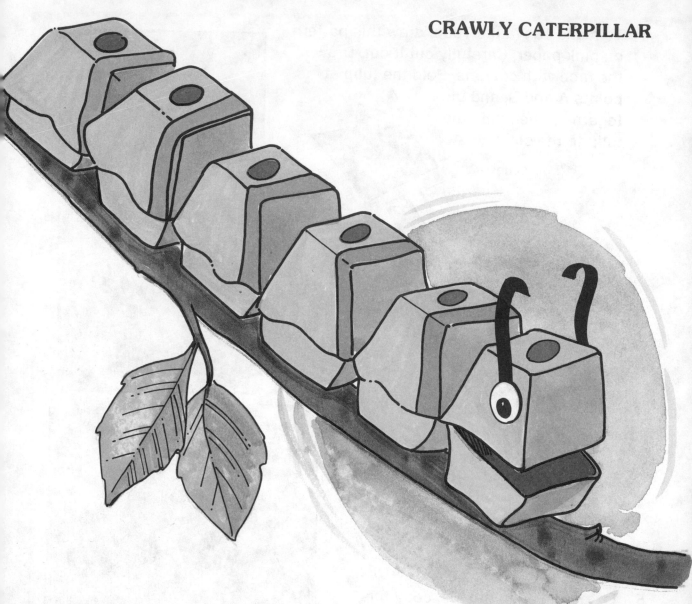

Here's what you need:

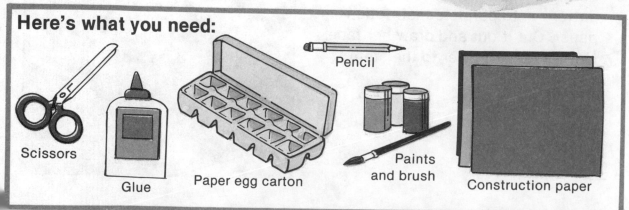

Scissors

Glue

Paper egg carton

Pencil

Paints and brush

Construction paper

Here's what you do:

1   Cut off the egg-carton cover. Then cut the carton lengthwise. Now cut one length apart into six separate cups.

2   Trim about ¼ " off the open end of each of the cups.

3   Glue five cups to the long strip of carton to make the caterpillar's body. Use the sixth to form the mouth. Trim and glue it at an angle into the first section.

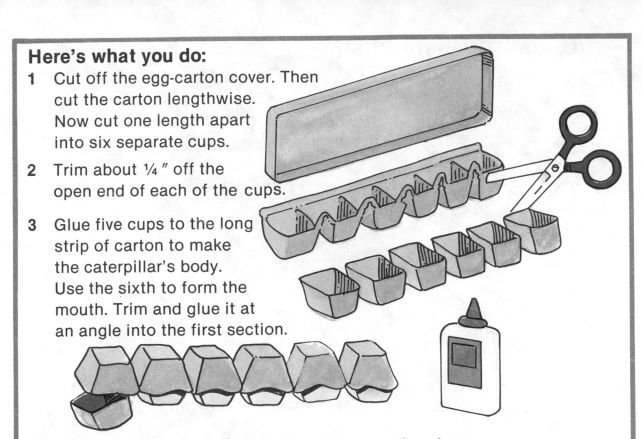

4   Paint the inside of the mouth red.

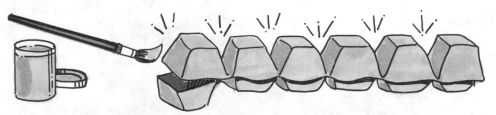

5   After glue has dried, paint the caterpillar a nice bright color. Let it dry. Then add eyes and colorful markings, using paint or construction paper.

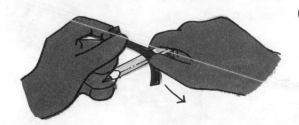

6   For the antennae, cut two strips of black paper. Curl each one around a pencil, as shown. Glue in place.

MILK-CARTON BIRDHOUSE

Here's what you need:

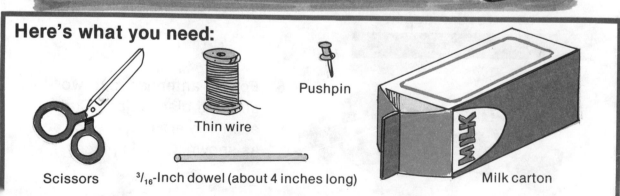

Scissors

Thin wire

Pushpin

³/₁₆-Inch dowel (about 4 inches long)

Milk carton

Here's what you do:

1 Wash and dry an empty milk carton. Cut away the front and side areas, as shown.

2 Make two small holes on either side of the carton, as pictured. Fit the dowel through the holes. This makes a nice perch for your feathered friends.

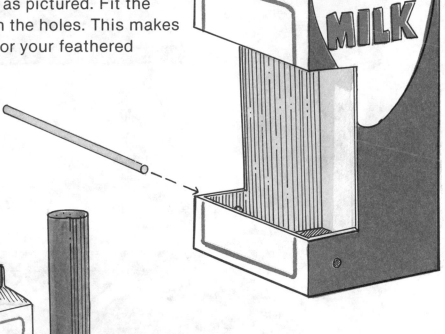

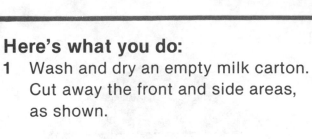

3 Now your birdhouse is ready to be attached to a pole or tree. Use a pushpin to make four holes in the back of the carton. Loop a length of wire through two of the holes. Do the same for the other two holes. Wrap the wires around the pole and tie tightly.

HOW TO EMPTY AN EGGSHELL

By hollowing out an egg, you can make pretty Easter ornaments that last for years. It takes some patience to learn this trick. But keep trying—the results are worth it. The next few pages show some eggshell projects you can try.

Here's what you need:

Fresh raw eggs

Pushpin

Bowl

Here's what you do:

1 Wash and dry the egg. Use a pushpin to make a small hole at each end of the egg.

2 Blow gently into one of the holes. Keep blowing until the inside of the egg oozes out into the bowl. Enlarge the holes a *little bit* at a time, but only if you need to. (Save the insides of the eggs to use for cooking.)

3 Carefully rinse out the egg-shell with water. Let it dry completely.

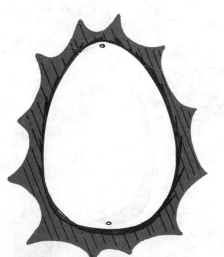

4 Now you're ready to paint designs on your eggshell. For some ideas, turn the page.

FABULOUS JEWELED EGGS

In many parts of the world, people give each other decorated eggs at Easter. The eggs are symbols of long life and good fortune.

Here's what you need:

Markers

Clear nail polish

Ribbon

Sequins

Magazines

Crayons

Paints and brushes

Glue

Glitter

Scissors

Hollow eggshells

Construction paper

Here's what you do:

1 Be sure your hollow eggshells are clean and dry. Work carefully.

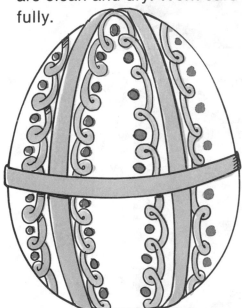

2 Draw or paint a design on the shell. Let the paint dry.

3 Glue on glitter, sequins, or gummed stars to get a rich jeweled look. You might want to glue on small pictures cut from magazines or shapes cut from construction paper.

4 Use your imagination to create some pretty eggs. The pictures on this page will give you some ideas. When your design is done and the glue is dry, give the egg a coat of clear nail polish to protect it.

JEWELED DISPLAY CASE AND STAND

Here is a pretty way to display your jeweled eggs.

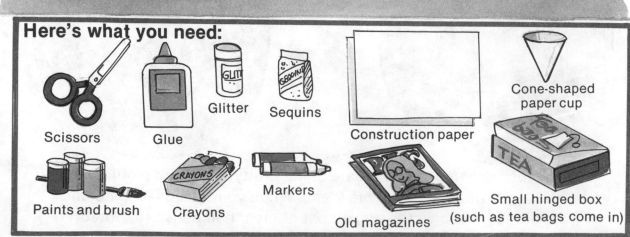

Here's what you need:

Scissors

Glue

Glitter

Sequins

Construction paper

Cone-shaped paper cup

Paints and brush

Crayons

Markers

Old magazines

Small hinged box (such as tea bags come in)

Here's what you do for the display stand:

1   Snip off the bottom of the paper cup. Make sure the decorated egg sits in the opening properly.
2   Now put the egg aside while you decorate the stand. Use your imagination! If you like, make a design that repeats the design on your egg.

Here's what you do for the case:

1   Open the lid of the box, gently fold it over, and make a small snip in the center.

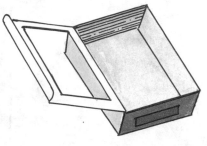

2   Then unfold the lid, and insert tip of scissors into slit. Cut out most of the lid area, until you have a frame the size you want. Remember to leave a fairly thick edge along the flap side of the lid.

3   Paint the box, inside and out. When the paint is dry, add pretty designs with sequins, glitter, pictures cut from magazines, bits of paper, crayons, and markers. If you like, make the design match the stand and egg. Now you're ready to set the egg on its stand inside the display case!

EASTER BASKET

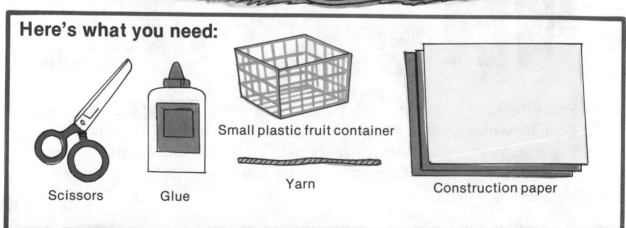

Here's what you need:

Scissors

Glue

Small plastic fruit container

Yarn

Construction paper

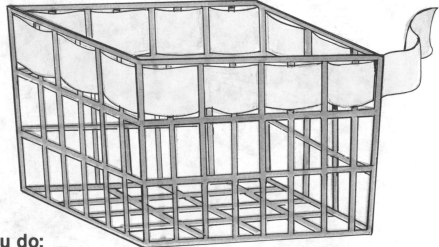

Here's what you do:

1 Cut strips of construction paper into long lengths. They should be wide enough to fit easily through the container's dividers. Weave the strips around the container. Use a different color for each row. Glue each strip closed when it circles the basket.

2 After the sides of the basket have all been woven, thread a short length of yarn to the basket for a handle.

3 Now you're ready to fill your basket with Easter eggs, jellybeans, or flowers.

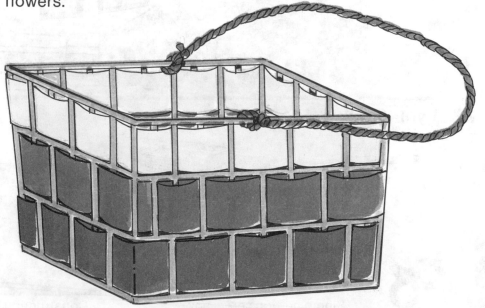

EASTER BUNNY PUPPET

Here's what you need:

Markers

Pencil

Crayons

White poster paint and brush

Construction paper

Glue

Scissors

Single-portion cereal box

Here's what you do:

1 Draw a line around the middle of an empty cereal box. The line should go across the front and two sides of the box. Carefully cut along the line.

2 Fold box in half, so there is a place for your fingers and thumb to go.

3 Now trace the box's outline on red paper, as shown.

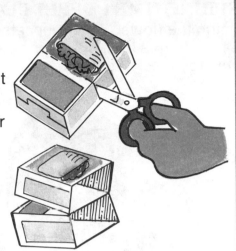

4 Cut out the rectangle and glue it to the box to make the inside of the bunny's mouth.

5 Give the rest of the rabbit a coat of white paint. Let dry, then give a second coat.

6 Cut out a shape for the bunny's ears and use crayons to color them. Glue the ears to the box. Cut out a shape from white paper for the teeth and glue into place.

7 Use a black marker and pink crayon to add the details of the eyes, nose, and teeth.

SPRINGTIME PUPPET PLAY

Using the flower finger puppets and the Easter bunny puppet described earlier in this book, you can make up a play all about spring! Here's how to make your stage.

Here's what you need:

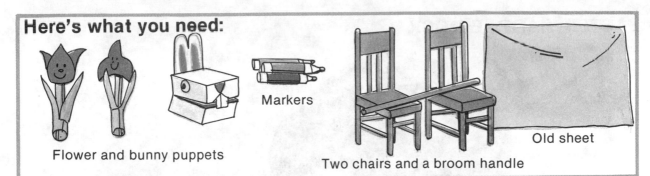

Flower and bunny puppets

Markers

Two chairs and a broom handle

Old sheet

Here's what you do:

1   Place the two chairs a few feet apart, back to back. Now put the broom handle across the backs of the chairs. Hang a sheet over the chairs and stick to complete your stage.

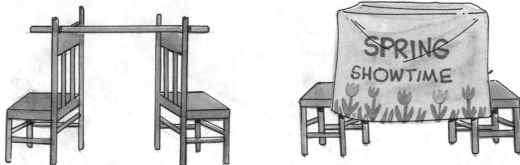

2   If you like, decorate your stage, using markers to draw a nice springtime scene.

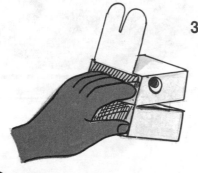

3   Now create a play all about the Easter bunny and his flowery friends!

EASTER WADDLE DUCK

Here's what you need:

Scissors

Pencil

Crayons or markers

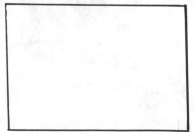

Metal fastener

White cardboard

Here's what you do:

1 Copy the duck pattern onto white cardboard and color, as shown. Then copy the circle pattern, which shows the legs. Now color the legs. Carefully cut out the duck and the circle.

2 Use a fastener to carefully make two small holes, as marked by X's.

3 Attach the legs to the duck's body with the fastener, as shown.

4 Hold the duck with one hand and roll it along on a table top. Watch your Easter duck waddle along!

FLUTTERING HONEYBEE

Here's what you need:

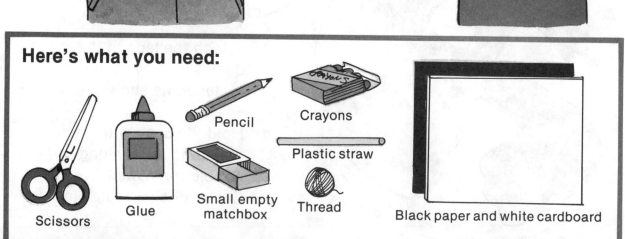

Scissors

Glue

Pencil

Crayons

Small empty matchbox

Plastic straw

Thread

Black paper and white cardboard

Here's what you do:

1 Make two small holes in matchbox drawer, where shown.

2 Then make two more holes opposite each other, as shown. Use a pencil point to enlarge the holes until a straw will fit snugly in them. Cut a short length of straw and fit it into the holes.

3 Copy the bee pattern onto cardboard. Color it. Then carefully cut the bee out.

4 For the antennae, glue two small strips of black paper in place.

5 Glue the matchbox drawer to the back of the bee. After glue dries, thread some string through the two holes, as shown.

6 To make your honeybee flutter, hold the string tight, relax the string, then hold tight again.

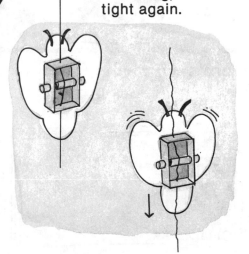

SPRING FLOWERS SCRAPBOOK

Here's a lovely way to save the first flowers of spring.

Here's what you need:

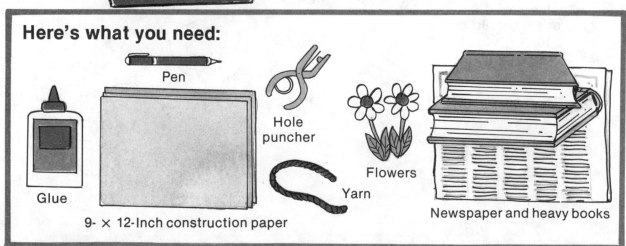

Pen

Glue

Hole puncher

Yarn

Flowers

9- × 12-Inch construction paper

Newspaper and heavy books

Here's what you do:

1 Lay your freshly picked flowers between sheets of newspaper. To press the flowers, place some heavy books on top of the newspapers. Wait at least one week before taking the flowers out.

2 To make the scrapbook, hold several sheets of construction paper together. Punch two holes through the sheets, as shown.

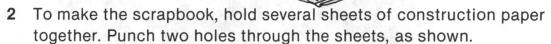

3 Thread a length of yarn through the holes and tie into a bow.

daisy

4 When the flowers are dry, gently glue each one to a page of your scrapbook. Then write the name of the flower shown on each page of the book.

PRETTY PLANTER

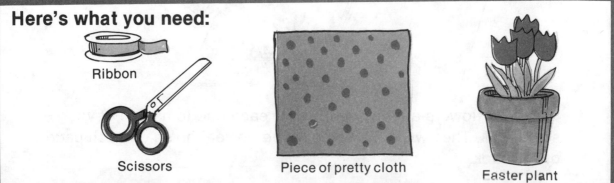

Here's what you need:

Ribbon

Scissors

Piece of pretty cloth

Easter plant

Here's what you do:

1 Place the potted plant on top of the piece of cloth. Trim cloth to form a circle.

2 Gather the cloth up and around the pot. Tuck the extra cloth into the top of the pot.

3 Tie a pretty ribbon around the pot. You now have a lovely Easter present for someone special.

Measurements

If you should need to find out the metric values of measurements given in these projects, this chart will help:

1 cup	=	240 milliliters
1 inch	=	25.4 millimeters or 2.5 centimeters
1 foot	=	30.5 centimeters